BLAZERS

SHARK ZONE

ZEBRA SHARK

Reading Consultant:
Barbara J. Fox
Reading Specialist
North Carolina State University

Content Consultant:
Jody Rake, member
Southwest Marine/Aquatic Educators' Association

CAPSTONE PRESS
a capstone imprint

Blazers is published by Capstone Press,
151 Good Counsel Drive, P.O. Box 669, Mankato, Minnesota 56002.
www.capstonepub.com

Books published by Capstone Press are manufactured with paper
containing at least 10 percent post-consumer waste.

Library of Congress Cataloging-in-Publication Data
Nuzzolo, Deborah.
  Zebra shark / by Deborah Nuzzolo.
    p. cm.—(Blazers. Shark zone)
  Summary: "Describes zebra sharks, their physical features, and their role in the ecosystem"—
Provided by publisher.
  Includes bibliographical references and index.
  ISBN 978-1-4296-5416-6 (library binding)
  1. Zebra shark—Juvenile literature. I. Title. II. Series.

  QL638.95.S92N893 2011
  597.3—dc22   2010024841

Editorial Credits

Christopher L. Harbo, editor; Juliette Peters, designer; Eric Manske, production specialist

Photo Credits

Alamy/David Fleetham, 15; imagebroker/Norbert Probst, 25; Stephen Frink Collection,
  18–19
Nature Picture Library/Jurgen Freund, 10–11
Peter Arnold/Biosphoto/Duclos Alexis, 5; Biosphoto/Gérard Soury, 16–17; Doug Perrine, 12;
  Kevin Aitken, 9
© SeaPics.com/Ingrid Visser, 26; Jeremy Stafford-Deitsch, 21; Mark Strickland, 12; Rodger
  Klein, cover, 28–29
Shutterstock/Ian Scott, 6–7; Kjersti Joergensen, 22–23

Artistic Effects

Shutterstock/artida; Eky Studio; Giuseppe_R

Printed in the United States of America in Stevens Point, Wisconsin.
092010   005934WZS11

TABLE OF CONTENTS

CHAPTER 1

ZEBRA OF THE SEA

A striped and spotted shark sits on the sandy seafloor. It lifts its head and smells the water. It spots a crab and bursts from the sand.

The crab tries to hide in a gap in a nearby **reef**. The shark swims along the reef and wiggles into the gap after the crab. The zebra shark snags its **prey**.

reef—a strip of rock, coral, or sand near the surface of the ocean

prey—an animal hunted by another animal for food

CHAPTER 2

SPOT THE HUNTER

Zebra sharks have long, slim bodies. They usually grow about 6 feet (1.8 meters) long. Large zebra sharks are almost 12 feet (3.7 m) long.

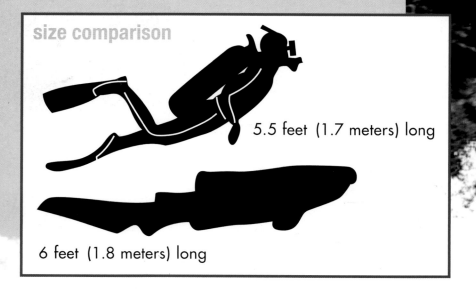

size comparison

5.5 feet (1.7 meters) long

6 feet (1.8 meters) long

SHARK FACT

Nearly half of a zebra shark's length is its tail. Zebra sharks use their long tails to move across the seafloor.

A zebra shark's color pattern changes over time. A young zebra shark has stripes. As the shark grows, the stripes become spots.

SHARK FACT

A zebra shark's color pattern helps it hide on the sandy seafloor.

denticles

A zebra shark's skin is rough like sandpaper. Its body is covered with hard **denticles**. These overlapping scales protect the shark's skin. As zebra sharks grow, they gain more denticles.

SHARK FACT

A denticle is no wider than the tip of a pencil.

denticle—a small, toothlike scale that covers a shark's skin for protection

Zebra sharks prop themselves up on the seafloor with their **pectoral fins**. This behavior helps them pump water into their mouths. The water flows out across their **gills** so they can breathe.

pectoral fin—the hard, flat limb on either side of a shark

gill—a body part that a fish uses to breathe

gills

pectoral fin

SHARK FACT

Zebra sharks spend the day on the seafloor. They become active at night when they hunt.

The zebra shark's skinny body helps it hunt. Zebra sharks easily slip into narrow cracks in the reef. They look for prey hidden in holes.

barbels

SHARK FACT

A zebra shark uses **barbels** near its mouth to find food. These fleshy feelers help the shark find prey it can't see.

barbel—a whiskerlike feeler on the head of some fish

Zebra sharks hunt small prey on the reef and in the sand. They eat snails and other **mollusks**. They also eat crabs, shrimp, and small fish.

mollusk—an animal with a soft body and no backbone

Zebra sharks have up to 34 small teeth in each jaw. Their teeth can crush the shells of prey.

CHAPTER 3

AT HOME IN THE SHALLOWS

Zebra sharks live in the Indian and western Pacific oceans. They like warm water. They swim in shallow areas close to shore.

Zebra Shark Range

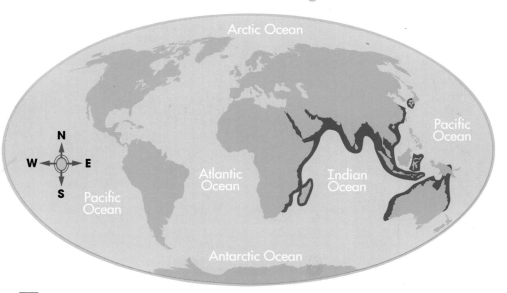

Arctic Ocean

N
W E
S

Pacific Ocean

Atlantic Ocean

Indian Ocean

Pacific Ocean

Antarctic Ocean

where zebra sharks live

Zebra sharks are important reef **predators**. Healthy reefs need a balance of predators and prey. Zebra sharks keep other animal populations from growing too large.

predator—an animal that hunts other
    animals for food

CHAPTER 4

ZEBRA SHARKS AND PEOPLE

Zebra sharks are not dangerous to people. But divers should avoid touching them. When zebra sharks become scared, they may bite.

SHARK FACT

People don't need to live near an ocean to see zebra sharks. Many aquariums and zoos display these amazing predators.

People are the biggest danger to zebra sharks. Some people catch zebra sharks for food. Other people catch them for sport.

SHARK FACT

Zebra shark fins are often used in a type of Chinese shark fin soup.

SHARK FACT

Zebra sharks depend on reefs for food. By protecting reefs, people also protect zebra sharks.

Zebra sharks are not **endangered**. But fishing activities along the shore could harm their population. By following fishing laws, people can protect the zebra shark.

endangered—at risk of dying out

Glossary

barbel (BAHR-buhl)—a whiskerlike feeler on the head of some fish

denticle (DEN-ti-kuhl)—a small, toothlike scale that covers a shark's skin for protection

endangered (in-DAYN-juhrd)—at risk of dying out

gill (GIL)—a body part that a fish uses to breathe; gills are the slits on the sides of a shark's head

mollusk (MOL-uhsk)—an animal with a soft body and no backbone

pectoral fin (PEK-tor-uhl FIN)—the hard, flat limb on either side of a shark

predator (PRED-uh-tur)—an animal that hunts other animals for food

prey (PRAY)—an animal hunted by another animal for food

reef (REEF)—a strip of rock, coral, or sand near the surface of the ocean

Read More

Doubilet, David, and Jennifer Hayes. *Face to Face with Sharks.* Washington, D.C.: National Geographic, 2009.

MacQuitty, Miranda. *Shark.* DK Eyewitness Books. New York: DK Pub., 2008.

Nuzzolo, Deborah. *Zebra Shark.* Sharks. Mankato, Minnesota: Capstone Press, 2009.

Internet Sites

FactHound offers a safe, fun way to find Internet sites related to this book. All of the sites on FactHound have been researched by our staff.

Here's all you do:

Visit *www.facthound.com*

Type in this code: 9781429654166

Check out projects, games and lots more at
www.capstonekids.com

Index